Freedom

Marc Maurer
Editor

Large Type Edition

A KERNEL BOOK
published by
NATIONAL FEDERATION OF THE BLIND

TABLE OF CONTENTS

Editor's Introduction

When we published our first Kernel Book fifteen years ago, who would have dreamed of the success of the project. As we approach the publication of volume thirty in the series, I am filled with gratitude and satisfaction when I contemplate the progress we are making together. I emphasize the word *together,* for this has truly been a partnership.

Some of you have been with us from the beginning; others have joined us more recently; and still others will be new with this volume. Likewise with the blind men and women who have shared the stories of their lives in these pages—some in that very first book and again along the way, others more recently, and some new just now.

All of us play a vital role in this undertaking —one that contributes to the well-being of

Marc Maurer, President
National Federation of the Blind

the tens of thousands of blind individuals living in their local communities throughout this vast country.

We've talked of many things together—from the color of the sun to whether old dogs can learn new tricks; from standing on one foot to coping with blizzards; from taking an African safari to remembering to feed the kittens; from making gray pancakes to grilling steaks over the hot charcoal.

No matter the subject the message is the same—in everything that matters we who are blind are just like you. We laugh, and we cry. We work, and we play. We worry about our children and take joy in our families. We participate in our churches, contribute to our neighborhoods, and hike in our parks.

You know these things because you've read our stories. And as you've come to know us, you proclaim our message.

In this present volume you'll meet more of us and learn new things about some of us you already know: a five-year-old who asks, "Mom, what does blind mean?"; a blind father who cries over spilled milk; a young man experiencing the joy and agony of first love; a child whose grandfather wouldn't take him fishing; and a woman racing on horseback through the Australian Outback.

This book will be released in late spring and certainly will be in full circulation by the fourth of July. That's the time when many of us will be thinking about the gift of *Freedom* those of us who are fortunate enough to live in this country share.

So as I put on my apron and join my fellow Americans around the barbeque grill, I will give thanks to God for this country and for all of you who are working with us to ensure that the blind share fully in the *Freedom* that belongs to all of us—especially to those who are prepared to work to preserve it, to protect it, to enhance it. I invite you to put on your apron and join me at the barbeque. Together we'll cook up a feast!

Marc Maurer
Baltimore, Maryland
2006

WHY LARGE TYPE?

The type size used in this book is 14-point for two important reasons: One, because typesetting of 14-point or larger complies with federal standards for the printing of materials for visually impaired readers, and we want to show you what type size is helpful for people with limited sight.

The second reason is that many of our friends and supporters have asked us to print our paperback books in 14-point type so they too can easily read them. Many people with limited sight do not use Braille. We hope that by printing this book in a larger type than customary, many more people will be able to benefit from it.

FREEDOM

by Marc Maurer

About a thousand years ago Lady Godiva became famous by accepting a challenge from her husband, the Earl of Mercia. She had asked him to lower the taxes he had imposed on the residents of Coventry. After long argument, the Earl finally agreed to reduce the level of taxation provided that his wife would ride her horse through the center of town at midday wearing no clothes. He said to her that she was a creature created by God, that God's creatures were beautiful, that there should be no shame in displaying this beauty, and that it was proper and admirable for the people of the town to observe God's handiwork.

To her husband's amazement, she accepted the challenge. On a prearranged day she rode through the town as required, accompanied by two maids on horseback, both fully clothed. The taxes were not merely reduced but eliminated.

In a later rendition of the legend, the element of blindness was added. In this version of the story, Lady Godiva had agreed to make her ride, but she asked that all residents of Coventry remain indoors so that she could do it in privacy. However, a tailor named Tom, consumed by curiosity and possibly baser passions, bored a hole in one of his shutters so that he could observe the ride. Because of this behavior, the tailor was "struck blind." The legend is the basis for the phrase "Peeping Tom."

Lady Godiva's efforts at tax reform are rarely remembered, but her famous ride is often depicted, and the story of "Peeping Tom" (which appears to be entirely fictional) has lasted for hundreds of years. The implications of incorporating blindness within this account are a matter of reflection for me as I serve in the principal leadership position of the National Federation of the Blind. However, I am also intrigued by the willingness of Lady Godiva to perform an unconventional act in quest of a just cause. I reflect that blindness must be confronted in unconventional ways if progress in surmounting its disadvantages is to be made and if we are truly to achieve freedom.

A few years ago I was describing the creation of the National Federation of the Blind Jernigan Institute, a building we were planning to construct at the National Center for the Blind in Baltimore. As a part of the presentation, I spoke about research and training projects we might undertake in this new facility.

In the course of my comments, I said that we might be able to build an automobile that the blind could use independently. The technologies that currently exist have already solved many of the problems that would need to be addressed to make this practical. In the computer programs of modern military aircraft, pattern recognition systems have been installed. Commercial planes can land (I am told) with no help from the pilot.

Robots have been built with object avoidance elements incorporated in their directional components. Global positioning systems can locate objects on the earth with astonishing accuracy. If all of these machines are combined, much of the work in constructing a vehicle for use by the blind will be done.

A driver interface that can be operated by the blind must be devised, but the prospects for doing so are good. The National Federation of the Blind has been working with Raymond Kurzweil to perfect a handheld reading machine, which will soon be available on the market. At the moment it can read black printed letters on white paper, but the ultimate objective is to build the mechanism so that it can recognize objects, describe scenes, distinguish human beings from other things, and serve as a mechanical kind of object detection device.

It is the beginning of machine-based optics or mechanical vision. Discussions regarding combining these technologies and constructing an interface that can be used by the blind within an automobile have taken place with a number of officials in the engineering schools of universities. Although the thinking involved in designing an automobile for the blind appears to be somewhat unconventional, many of the people considering the problem approach the matter as a straightforward engineering task. However, psychology cannot be forgotten. Americans do love their cars.

On a recent afternoon as I was sitting in my chair daydreaming, my mind drifted. It seemed to me that I was visiting a friend in California and that I was examining his automobile in the driveway, a brand new

Lincoln Continental convertible. Because I have worked as a mechanic in the years before I attended college, I have come to know about the internal structure of automobiles and the controls that operate them. I slid behind the wheel, and I touched the buttons, switches, and levers.

Although I have become knowledgeable about the controls for many automobiles, the ones in this machine seemed unfamiliar to me, and I wondered what they did. I pressed one of the buttons at random, and I was startled when the car began to move.

The vehicle rolled from the driveway into the street, a very quiet residential thoroughfare. As I sat in the driver's seat, the wheel turned to the right, and so did the car. As it headed for the intersection (the cross street was very heavily traveled, with much traffic) the car picked up speed, and I became more nervous. I stepped on the brake pedal, but nothing happened. I tried it again, but still nothing happened. As I could hear the noise of the crossing traffic increase, I began to mutter to myself "how do you get this thing to stop?" By the time I got to the last word, I spoke it aloud with tremendous force.

Imagine my astonishment; the Lincoln responded to my voice; it stopped. I hadn't realized that one of the methods for controlling the machine was to give it oral instructions. I decided to experiment. I told the car to turn around and go home. The machine obeyed; soon we were safely back in the driveway of my friend.

My daydream was at an end, but I was curious (maybe even a little disappointed) at my reaction to it. In getting back to the driveway, my overwhelming feeling was one of relief. Cars can be dangerous, and I was quite worried about having one nominally under my control that I could not manipulate with ease. I think that this is a sensible attitude, but it does lack a certain sense of adventure.

Inasmuch as I have been blind all of my life, I am aware that blind people are very frequently told that the adventurous side of life is not for them. I, however, have very often rejected such assertions. In the process of seeking new experiences, I have hiked in the mountains, climbed rock faces, rebuilt automobile engines, represented clients in court, water-skied, handled an arc welder, and learned to use an axe. Nevertheless, I was afraid of the automobile. I am pleased that it was all a daydream because I will now have the time to develop the courage needed to address the fear.

In one of his stories, O. Henry said "Life is made up of sobs, sniffles, and smiles—with sniffles predominating." As I look at it, I think that fear, frustration, and joy must be added to the mixture.

In my work with the National Federation of the Blind, I spend a good deal of my time helping people overcome the fear, surmount the frustrations, and attain the joy. I have learned as much as I could about blindness in general and about my own blindness in particular. The subject is not new to me, and sometimes I believe I have learned what there is to know. However, I must keep an open mind because I am subject to the same misunderstandings that other people have about blindness.

Can I dream of a time when I will be able to use a piece of equipment safely and effectively that weighs more than three thousand pounds? Will I be able to overcome my timidity and grasp the opportunities that come my way? Will I be able to inspire others to accept challenges that they now believe are beyond them? I will with your help—with your understanding and your belief in what we in the National Federation of the Blind are doing.

Are blind people different from the sighted? In some ways we are, but in all that is important, there are no distinctions. We hope and dream—plan and work. We long for positive experience and success for our families. And if we do our work well, we will find a way to reduce taxes, build our communities, and shape new technologies that make us independent and give us freedom. Your faith in us makes this a practical possibility.

Junior Prom

by Dave Hyde

David Hyde is a longtime leader in the National Federation of the Blind of Oregon. With perspective and sparkle he looks back to his high school days and his first love. Here is what he has to say:

To be young and in love—is there any memory as warm as that special person for whom you would do anything within the realm of possibility and be more than willing to expand the realm? It's even more exciting as a blind teenager to learn that a sighted girl likes you. At sixteen, I was a junior in high school on the Oregon coast. Over the summer I met a girl named Beth who lived about ninety minutes away. And I fell in love.

Since neither of us drove (she didn't have a car, and I was blind), we saw each other when we could and conducted our relationship over the telephone. The phone would ring, and there on the other end would be Beth's mellifluous coloratura soprano voice, exuding warmth and affection.

We talked about everything; no subject was off-limits. Beth was smart and talented—and she was mine. I sent her presents, and I saved my allowance and the money I made over the summer to pay the mounting phone bills. Both of our families were poor, but that didn't matter to us.

When my fellow students started talking about the Junior Prom, I called Beth. I desperately wanted her to go with me. I was afraid that she would say no—but I was just as afraid she would say yes. After talking with her mother, she agreed to come. I was so happy, so proud, and so scared. Our telephone conversations then centered around her dress. She had found one in

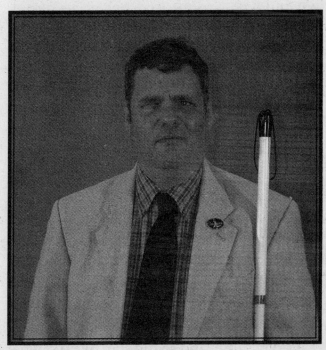

Dave Hyde

her price range and told me all about it. I couldn't wait to see it on her, and I anxiously called the florist to order a corsage to match it perfectly.

I planned the weekend meticulously. She would come in on the bus, and we would pick her up and take her to our home. We'd spend Friday evening together, and Saturday we would get ready for the prom. I'd take her out to dinner (I had made reservations at a restaurant near the dance) and had arranged with my uncle for a ride to and from. I certainly didn't want to have my mother take us to the prom! Sunday would be free, and she would go back on the bus Monday morning. Everything was set.

Friday came, and so did she. We did what we always did: talked, listened to music, and held hands. All was right with the world. On Saturday in the late afternoon she did her hair and put on her dress. It was ruffled with spaghetti straps and was the first formal she had ever worn. I pinned the corsage on her (with some help), and in my humble opinion, she was the loveliest girl in the world.

The night was magical. I felt dashing in my suit and tie. My uncle picked us up and drove us to the restaurant. They had our reservation, we ate dinner, and I proudly paid the bill. We then walked to the prom ballroom, had some cake and punch, and even though I was not a good dancer, we danced. Everything was right. About midnight my uncle picked us up and drove us home. As we talked in the living room, she told me how much fun she had had, what a marvelous prom it had been, and how happy she was to have gone with me.

Sunday came, and the formal and the suit were packed away. The corsage was in its box in the refrigerator, and jeans and t-shirts were the uniform of the day. We took a walk and talked about the prom, about us, and about how much we cared for each other. I was sixteen, and my heart was whole and full. I decided to talk about the future. I said that I was going to go to college in a couple of years and that I loved her and would like to find a way to make our relationship permanent.

It got very quiet. I am sure that the universe expanded and contracted at least once, which only takes around eighteen billion years. Then she said that she wasn't sure. She said she liked me, and I was nice and had treated her better than anyone ever had. That was the first shoe—the other was in the air. Then she said that she just didn't know if she could go through life with a blind man.

I couldn't fight that battle at sixteen; I did the right thing and thanked her for being so honest. I told her that I understood—although I didn't.

I made it through the rest of Sunday and took her to the bus on Monday. Then I went home and cried. I cried for myself, but I also cried for her. Blindness was part of me, and anyone who loved me couldn't doubt me as much as she did. My heart felt empty. I really wondered if I was lovable at all.

Beth and I lost track of each other. I ran into her once more after the prom, but things weren't the same. I stopped calling and writing. After a while she became something that had happened and was now over. I finished high school and went to college. I finished college and met Nancy.

Nancy is a contralto, not a soprano. I never took her to a prom. We talk about everything and have for more than twenty-seven years. We love each other, fight with each other, and support each other. Blindness is not an issue. She expects me to do things independently and to be successful. When I asked her to be my wife, there was no question about whether she could go through life with a blind husband.

Over the years I have made mistakes because of being careless, unobservant, or downright dumb—and Nancy is more than willing to help me remember them. But it is clear to me that she understands these mistakes are not because I am blind. She is smart, fun, warm, and caring.

The difference is that she understands blindness as a characteristic, which means that it isn't an excuse for anything. If I don't know how I'm going to accomplish a task, we talk about it. She frequently has ideas that I hadn't thought of. This is how a good partnership works.

The prom was a long time ago. But I am still in love. It's different now, since there is a great deal of mutual respect between my wife and me. Now I know when the phone rings, it is a friend saying hello or someone who wants to sell me storm windows or contribute to a good cause. And my long-distance bills take a much smaller bite out of my income than they did when I was sixteen.

CRYING OVER SPILLED MILK

by Parnell Diggs

We often say that the real problem of blindness is not the lack of eyesight but is the lack of understanding about it. The truth of that statement is born out forcefully in this story by Parnell Diggs. Here is what he has to say:

My long white cane extended, I walked into a hotel restaurant one Thursday with my wife and nineteen-month-old son. I asked for a Braille menu, and Kim and I began talking. Our family was being observed (I soon learned) by two ladies at a nearby table.

Jordan played with his toys while we made decisions about lunch. Kim and Jordan were having the buffet, and Daddy (everybody knows I love a good sandwich) was instructed to put Jordan in his highchair as soon as I had ordered off of the menu.

From his highchair, Jordan was unable to disturb the drinks I had made certain were across the table beyond his reach. "I bet he wants his milk," a lady from the nearby table said striding over and placing the styrofoam cup in front of my son.

I grabbed the cup and gave Jordan a sip of milk. "Say thank you," I prodded knowing the plastic lid and straw were not designed to prevent spills by toddlers. Moving the cup again out of harm's way, I sat down and awaited Kim's return from the buffet line.

The low-pitched thud against a container full of liquid, the soaked tablecloth, and the embarrassed laughter of the two ladies on the other side of the highchair created an awkwardness that could have been avoided if the two ladies had not been so well intentioned.

Parnell Diggs

As a favor to me, they had gently placed Jordan's cup in front of him a second time on their way out of the restaurant not realizing that I had deliberately placed it where he couldn't reach it. I jumped up, "Yeah, pull him away from the table," one of them said as I checked Jordan's clothes, which were still dry.

Could they have imagined that I am a self-employed attorney with a wife who works at home? In their wildest dreams, could they have realized that I was there to preside at a business meeting that weekend that would be attended by 350 persons?

Put a white cane in my hand, and I became a blind man who didn't know that my son couldn't reach his milk. "You may want to get help," they suggested. "It's running onto the floor." I guess they figured out why I had put Jordan's milk where he couldn't reach it.

A sighted parent may have done the same thing as opposed simply to holding a child's hands down. Without a "sippy cup," I made a judgment call, and they had made a judgment call too. They knew that I was blind.

Rather than assuming that I had put the cup out of reach on purpose because my nineteen-month-old son could not yet hold that type of cup, the ladies who had been observing us assumed that I, being blind, didn't know where I had put it.

This spilled milk was definitely worth crying over, but not because we had to change tables and ask for more milk. In their minds, my life experience was irrelevant. Jordan (though still a toddler) had already exceeded the competence of his blind father.

The ladies who would give Jordan his milk so he could spill it would not give me a job so I could buy it.

The tears I shed are a result of the knowledge that my son will very soon come to know that people think his father is incapable of providing for himself, his family, and incapable even of doing something so fundamental as giving his son his milk.

Jordan will be told that he is less fortunate than other children are because his dad is blind—but thanks to the National Federation of the Blind he won't believe it. Blindness is not a tragedy. With proper training and opportunity, blindness can be reduced to the level of a mere physical nuisance. I am determined that this is the message of blindness that my son will hear most.

MOM, WHAT DOES BLIND MEAN?

by Pauletta Feldman

There are a few subjects in our society that even the most confident parents find difficult to discuss with their children. Trying to explain or answer a question about sex or death to an inquisitive five-year-old, for example, can leave us stammering. Fortunately, there are many places parents can turn to for help. But what do you do if you have a blind child? Where do you turn for guidance when your child asks, "Mom, what does blind mean?" By the time her son Jamie asked that question, Pauletta Feldman was prepared—she had been in the National Federation of the Blind's parents group since Jamie had been a toddler. Here is what she has to say:

It wasn't until my son, Jamie, was five years old that he finally asked me, "Mom, what does *blind* mean?" We'd used the word blind in conversation, and he'd certainly heard it from other people. But we hadn't really discussed blindness or its implications with Jamie. Maybe we were just "chicken" and putting off the inevitable.

However, we had decided that we would handle discussions of blindness with Jamie as we had handled discussions of sex with our older children: when they started asking questions, we felt they were ready to be told the facts.

So that day at naptime when Jamie asked about blindness, I sucked in a big breath and summoned my courage. "*Blind* means that you can't see with your eyes," I said. "I can see things with my eyes. I can see the trees and the birds and all of the other things I tell you about. But you see things in a different way than with your eyes. You use your smart fingers and your smart ears." He was quite

Pauletta's son Jamie

satisfied with that answer and didn't pursue the subject further that day. However in the days to come, he would ask questions again. The kind of questions he asked led me to believe that, in his mind, he wasn't the one that was different. I was! In a way, it was like his first notion of differences among people was of how they were different from him, rather than how he was different from them. I liked that—I liked how self-confident and self-loving he was.

For a while, Jamie seemed to think that everybody we knew was blind and that there were just a few people who could see. He began asking about person after person in our family and among our friends to sort out who was blind and who was not. Gradually he came to realize that he knew more people who could see than who could not. I'm so thankful that we knew other blind children and adults so that as this realization dawned on him, he did not feel isolated or alone. The blind people that we knew were really neat people. They were friends and fun to be with, just like our other friends. They were people that Jamie really liked, and he could feel good about having something in common with them.

Jamie began school and loved learning to read Braille. He became very interested in how sighted people read. Then he began asking of everyone we knew whether they read with their fingers or with their eyes.

During the past two years since facing that first question, there have been many incidents that have brought both hidden tears and silent laughter as we have gone through Jamie's formation of opinions about blindness. There was the day that he came home from school very indignant because a teacher had mentioned that he couldn't see. He said, "I told her that I can too see! I can see the light!" Another day, as he and his brother sat at the kitchen table doing homework, he asked accusingly, "Is Don doing his homework with his eyes?" And he laid his face on his Brailled worksheet and said, "Then I'm doing my homework with my eyes too!" He decided that someday he was going to go to school with his brother and then he would be able to read print because they didn't teach Braille there.

As Jamie has gotten older, some of his responses to his blindness have begun to be tinged with sadness. One day we read a little book called "Corky the Blind Seal," about a seal in a zoo who lost his sight. The next day as he got off the school bus, he said, "I want to be a bus driver when I grow up!" My heart ached, and I just said," I bet driving a school bus is fun, too." But when we got in the house, he confessed. "I know I can't be a bus driver. Blind people can't drive, and I'm blind. I'm glad I'm blind, Mom. I just wish I could be blind like Corky the seal was blind, because he got to see first." He asked if it was nice to be able to see, and I said that it was.

We talked about how he could see what I see using his other senses, like when we went to the ocean he could feel the water, taste its saltiness, hear its waves, and smell it, too. He liked knowing that there were things that even people who were sighted actually couldn't see, like the wind—that we had to hear it and feel it to know it was there just like he did.

I've always wanted Jamie to feel good about himself. I haven't wanted him to think that there is anything wrong with the way he is. I haven't been able to bring myself to tell Jamie that, according to some people, there is something wrong with being blind. Maybe I'll regret this someday, but I figure in time he'll learn. I hope he will come to me with his questions then and that I'll be able to answer them. To me, blindness is a difference, a source of sadness sometimes and inconvenience at others, but there's nothing wrong with it.

Life is a journey of self-discovery. I want Jamie's journey to bring self-love with the discovery of his many potentials and capabilities as well as his personal limitations. We all have to face certain limitations. It's how we cope with them that really matters. So far, Jamie has always managed to find a silver lining for every one of his clouds, to compensate for each limitation with a special strength. Why just last week he said, "Mom, aren't you glad I'm blind and have such smart fingers and can read Braille? You can't read Braille with your fingers! You have to use your eyes."

Do You Want to Run?

by Melody Lindsey

Melody Lindsey is a longtime leader of the National Federation of the Blind. She lives in Michigan, where she directs a training center for people who are blind. Recently she visited an Australian sheep farm. There, in the wide-open expanses of the Outback, she found new insights for her work with blind adults. Here is what she has to say:

As the train pulled out of the Melbourne, Victoria, station, it picked up speed quickly. Before long, scenes from the countryside rushed past us almost in a blur. This train was a high-speed train that made stops between Melbourne and Sydney.

The conductor entered the car and began collecting tickets from the passengers. "And where are we going today, Miss?" he asked.

"My destination is "The Rock." Can you let me know when we arrive there please?" I asked.

"No worries, mate," he replied jovially. "We should be arriving around 12:30 this afternoon—four hours from now."

A couple minutes later a woman came through the car dispensing tea and other breakfast items. I have never had so much tea as I had since I arrived in Australia one week earlier. This morning I purchased a cup of tea and settled in for the long trip.

Two days earlier, after the session of the World Blind Union had ended for the day, I began talking to people about the various activities one could do around Australia. I had come to this conference in Melbourne

Melody Lindsey

as a delegate from the United States Rehabilitation Services Administration to the World Blind Union forum for women. I had a few days in which I could be a tourist and wanted to find a vacation I could take where I would meet and spend time with everyday Australians.

At dinner that night a couple attending the meetings of the World Blind Union told me about their itinerary for the next three weeks in Australia. One of the activities that caught my interest was a visit they planned to make to a sheep farm in New South Wales.

The name of the place was Hanericka Farm Stays, and I called the next day to make a reservation. The man who answered the phone took my information and told me to get off the train at the stop called "The Rock." "Okay," I said. "What is your address so I can tell the cab driver where I need to go?" The man laughed and informed me that there were no cabs and that they would have someone pick me up from the train.

Next I asked, "Should I call you from the train station?" For some reason I pictured it to be a bustling train station, similar to Melbourne, with numerous telephones and vending machines where a weary traveler could by coffee or tea.

The man informed me that there were no phones and that all the station would be was a small platform. This was somewhat unsettling to me because then what I imagined was a vast desert with one lone train track running through it and a small platform sitting in the midst of rolling sand dunes and tumbleweed. Of course, I imagined poisonous snakes awaiting my arrival under the platform.

In actuality, when I arrived at "The Rock" a young woman named Julie was waiting for me on the platform and introduced herself as the hostess for Hanericka Farm Stays. We got into the car and headed down a two-lane road toward the sheep farm. The train platform for "The Rock" was situated in the middle of a small farming community with houses and buildings scattered along the tracks. Oh, and by the way, there were no snakes waiting to greet me either.

When we got to the farmhouse where I would stay, Julie prepared lunch and gave a short tour of the place. I ate lunch that day with Julie; Yoshi, a farm worker; and Neville, whose children ran various aspects of the farm. It was the end of November, which is the close of spring in Australia. It was very warm and dusty and reminded me of some of the scenes described in the *Australian Destiny* books by Sandy Dengler that I had read a couple of years earlier.

Although the weather was nice, the perpetual presence of swarms of flies was somewhat disconcerting. I was given some spray to deal with these nuisances that I carried with me almost everywhere I went.

I told Neville the next day at lunch that I had a suggestion for improving the farm. "Oh," he said, "What is it?"

"Get rid of the flies," I said, to which he said that the best way to do that would be to take a dead sheep and put it outside the door so that the flies would be attracted to it and not me. Needless to say, everyone around us thought we engaged in such charming dinner conversation. We did enjoy discussing the American and Australian political systems and other cultural differences and similarities.

After eating breakfast the next morning, Yoshi, who did various chores around the farm, told me that his assignment for the day was to be my tour guide. We went down to the barn and went for a morning ride on two horses.

I referred to Yoshi as the Japanese cowboy from Australia, because that's exactly what he was. I asked him why someone from

Japan would want to be a cowboy and how would that person end up in Australia to follow his dreams. "I always associated cowboys with the Wild West in the United States," I said.

Yoshi was very patient in answering me. "I always loved the open space you find in the outdoors. I liked riding horses and knew that I wanted a job that would combine the two. Japan is a very crowded country with little countryside, so I did some research into cowboy jobs in the United States. There was nothing. But then I learned about a place in Australia that was looking for a farmhand. I applied and came to Australia and have never looked back. In fact, I am applying for my Australian citizenship because this is where I want to live the rest of my life. I figure I only have one soul, and I should make the best use of it that I can."

After riding in silence for a few minutes, Yoshi asked, "Do you want to run?"

"Can we really?" I asked eagerly.

"Sure," he said, and both of our horses broke into a run. It was so exhilarating to feel the breeze through my hair and to know that someone was not questioning my ability to enjoy a run while on horseback.

It struck me while we were running: Isn't this what we should be asking blind people who come to us for rehabilitation training? How many times do we limit people in learning how to run because of our irrational fear of liability or because of our low expectations? Blind people should be challenged to learn to run so that they will know that feeling of exhilaration and confidence.

The next day before returning to Melbourne, Yoshi and I went for one last horseback ride. It was windy, which was both good and bad. Good because it kept the flics away, and bad because Yoshi and I could not hear each other as well.

Yoshi asked, "Do you want to run?" And we took off running across the field.

Suddenly, I heard Yoshi yelling something, but I could not hear him because he was getting farther away. Then, I figured out that my horse must have been running the wrong way. It was up to me to get my horse stopped and turned in the right direction—in other words back under control.

Again I thought: Isn't this what we should be doing with the blind students who come to us for training? Shouldn't we be teaching them to handle problems that arise independently and competently? And if we always avoid problem situations, how will people learn that they can handle them successfully? Wow, I thought, Yoshi would make a great teacher!

That afternoon I left Hanericka Farm Stays feeling that I had made some friends and had learned a great deal about the Australian way of life.

On the train trip back to Melbourne, I reflected on my holiday at the sheep farm. What had made it so refreshing and invigorating? In recounting the events from the past two days, I decided that what made it such a wonderful vacation was the fact that it was always assumed that I could do something.

Of course, there were some people, including the children, who had questions about my blindness, but it seemed to me that they also assumed that I had other interests in addition to blindness. Julie said to me once, "It's good for the kids to spend time around you since they have never seen a blind person. I think that they'll learn that you are not as different as they might think."

I do not know if I will ever get a chance to go back to the sheep farm. I hope so because since I was there at the end of November and the sheep shearing does not begin until March or April, I have not learned the process involved in shearing sheep. If I do receive the opportunity, this would be the perfect place to do it because the expectation is there that a blind person not only can do it, but also can do it well.

WHEN BLINDNESS MATTERED

by Daniel B. Frye

All of us are influenced by and absorb the attitudes of others even when those attitudes don't seem to fit with our own personal experiences. This is particularly true for children and is one of the reasons why these Kernel Books are so important to the National Federation of the Blind. Dan Frye reflects on how he rose above the limited expectations he faced as a child growing up in rural South Carolina. Here is what he has to say:

My sister Debbie and I were sent to live with our paternal grandparents in the low country of South Carolina following the death of our father in July of 1980. Our mother had succumbed to critical injuries two years earlier after a serious car accident.

Our flight from Texas to South Carolina during the early hours of that summer morning represents my first vivid memory of travel on an airplane.

To this day the sunrise I saw during that flight remains the most spectacular phenomenon I have ever seen: a brilliant orange-red ball of flames sitting alone on what appeared to be an infinite field of deepest, coldest blue sky. We were served French toast and given a packet of Eastern Airlines playing cards. After a few hours we landed in South Carolina to start our new lives in the country.

We lived with our grandparents in their two-bedroom house on an acre of farm land in the Cedar Creek community, some ten miles outside of Nichols, a small town of about 10,000 people. In addition to the house, my grandparents owned an old tobacco barn, a wash house where laundry was done, a pump house for the well, and a chicken coop to mark the property line at the back of the farm.

Dan Frye

They had a garden in which they grew everything imaginable, including peanuts and the largest watermelons I have ever seen. The front of the house had a conventional raised porch with gray rotting planks of wood, a large evergreen tree that offered abundant shade across the circular dirt driveway, and a set of black and red rusting lawn chairs that kept the shade tree company year-round.

Our place was about a quarter of the way down the wandering four-mile dirt road that ran in front of our property. Only several years after I left my grandparents' custody was the road assigned a name by local officials in order for the Cedar Creek community to become part of the 911 emergency system.

The Cedar Creek Baptist Church and Mr. Stanley's country store sat at the two ends of the dirt road, and both places were frequently a destination for my little sister and me since getting lost was virtually impossible if you faithfully followed the side of the road until it ended. Despite the considerably longer distance from our house, Mr. Stanley's store was our favorite destination.

We would buy two bottles of Pepsi Cola and two Moon Pies for a dollar. We'd temper the stifling heat and forget the clouds of gnats that perpetually inhabited South Carolina's low country by drinking our Pepsis and dipping our toes in the creek at the side of the dirt road halfway home from the store.

The aroma of simple home cooking, animals at pasture, and the diverse scents of nature were prominent among my first impressions of our new neighborhood. On the first Sunday morning of our permanent residence with our grandparents, for instance, my grandmother took my sister and me out to the chicken coop to be unwitting witnesses to the summary execution of that day's dinner.

She exhibited a calm, matter-of-fact attitude as she efficiently wrung the necks of two birds and then undertook the smelly and distasteful process of removing their feathers. Later, though, more pleasant odors of frying chicken and weekly baking wafted throughout the house and onto the front porch, which attracted my attention and diverted my mind from the recent violent encounter to which the Sunday birds had been subjected.

Across the yard a large pile of rotting potatoes lay, easily identifiable from a distance by smell, waiting to be carted across the road by the two newest members of the household and dropped into the adjacent woods to be returned to nature. In the garden we would seek cleansing refuge from that task by inhaling the natural scent of freshly tilled ground and ripening strawberries.

Finally, I particularly remember the distinctive sulfuric taste and smell of the water that came from the well and that could be mitigated only by chilling in the refrigerator for several hours. Suffice it to say, we had been installed in an entirely new world, quite different from the suburban childhood we had spent in the outskirts of Austin, Texas.

After about a week our status as visiting grandchildren changed, and we adopted a routine more reflective of a family. Unfortunately for me, this development made it abundantly clear that my grandparents, being part of the broader society, had limited expectations about the abilities of a blind child. When the family rose at six to harvest butterbeans from the garden, avoiding the heat of midday, I was expressly told that I could not join in this chore.

I protested mightily but was led to believe that I was slow and would inhibit productivity. Instead, I was told to sit under the evergreen and shell beans as they were brought to me, an enviable duty for one who disliked physical exertion. Nevertheless, I knew it was an unfair privilege, and I felt quite dispirited about the assignment.

Similarly, I was prohibited from performing most domestic chores, with the exception of rinsing dishes and scrubbing the bathroom. My sister, on the other hand, was asked to assume work responsibilities for both of us.

The sibling resentment that this unfair treatment created became palpable, and my effort to explain that I did not enjoy the privileges I was receiving was understandably not fully believed or comprehended by my ten-year-old little sister. During these times I spent alone either in the guilty comfort of close proximity to our window air-conditioning unit in the house or out under the evergreen tree, I first realized that blindness mattered.

The disparate treatment that we received from our grandparents was not limited to the performance of household and farming tasks only; it also had recreational implications.

My grandfather established the tradition of taking each of his grandchildren fishing for a day. The two would leave at four in the morning, carry the boat down to the river, and fish until late afternoon. They would share a lunch of Vienna sausages, crackers, and water. Most of all, though, they shared time together. Debbie had her turn; so did everybody else. I frequently inquired when it would be my turn and was always promised that we would manage the trip sometime.

Ultimately, when Debbie and my grandfather were making their second trip, my grandmother confided that he didn't want to be responsible for a blind person on the water. In retrospect I am not persuaded that I ever really yearned to spend a day on a smelly boat with a limited diet and the prospect of getting my hands dirty, but at the time it seemed a special opportunity denied. At that moment blindness mattered.

In September, my grandmother took me aside and explained that I would be going to the South Carolina School for the Deaf and

Blind in Spartanburg, some 300 miles north of home. Oh, how I cried. I argued that I didn't want to leave Debbie alone so soon after coming to a new home. I explained that my parents had enrolled me in public schools since the third grade and that I had been coping well. I swore that I'd be a good boy if they'd just let me stay at home.

Despite these petitions the decision was made, and we drove to the red hills of the upperstate, where I resumed my education. Again, with the objective counsel of time and distance, I can see that this arrangement had advantages for me, but they were not the advantages that my grandparents perceived, and ultimately it was clear that blindness mattered.

Finally I remember telling my grandmother that I wanted to be a lawyer since my father had told me that being a policeman wasn't practical if you couldn't drive a car. I told her that Dad, a policeman himself, had told me that I'd have to work really hard and save lots of money in order to go to college. She lovingly but firmly doused these dreams with cold water, suggesting that I'd better plan to make brooms or, if I were lucky, hope to be a preacher in the Baptist church, where you could find jobs without formal theological training.

My grandfather's pessimism about my academic aspirations was more brusquely conveyed when he observed with exasperation that all I did was read "those damn Braille books"—an ironic complaint since I wasn't allowed to use my hands for harvesting, fishing, or other meaningful contributions towards the well-being of the family. By summer's end, I was certain that blindness mattered.

One of the unanticipated advantages of going to the school for the blind was my immediate exposure to the work of the National Federation of the Blind (NFB). South Carolina affiliate leaders established the nation's first junior chapter of the NFB on the campus at Cedar Springs, and I quickly took an interest in the chapter and also in the activities and philosophy of our national movement. I cannot fully convey the self-confidence and emotional security I absorbed from reading the empowering banquet speeches of Dr. Kenneth Jernigan given to me by organization leaders.

I benefited immeasurably from the indulgent mentoring of older blind men and women who cared enough to devote some time to affirming my dreams. I began to seek permission to stay away from home on the weekends and ultimately managed to emancipate myself from my grandparents' custody. The NFB had given me the gift of belief in myself and the promise that hard work could yield unlimited personal accomplishment.

Upon reflection, I feel a measure of pride that I was gradually able to persuade my grandmother of my capacity to help the family. When my sister and grandfather went on yet another fishing trip, incidentally an activity that Debbie never really enjoyed, my grandmother asked me to help her pick butterbeans in the garden.

She was pleasantly surprised that I could effectively empty the bushes, even finding beans among the leaves that she had missed because of relying on vision. I never minded aching muscles or being drenched in perspiration. I wished only that my grandmother had possessed the courage to allow me to help in these basic ways with my grandfather present, but that was probably a more complicated request than simply sorting out the truth about blindness.

Emboldened by the philosophy and programs of the NFB, I learned that my early conclusion that blindness matters was correct. More important, however, is the fact that our collective efforts are helping to make certain that blindness matters less and less in the larger scheme of things.

Today I am employed as the National Advocate for the Association of Blind

Citizens of New Zealand (ABC NZ), where I am professionally charged with making sure that blindness doesn't matter quite so much. Occasionally I recollect that first remembered flight and believe that the freedom I felt seeing that amazing sunrise and limitless sky has largely come to fruition in my life.

I have no doubt, though, that blindness will always, to some extent, influence my experiences and color my perceptions. I have learned that, for those of us who cannot see, blindness is an integral part of our character as human beings. I have come to understand that blindness will always matter but that what matters most is the way we come to understand blindness.

CUTTING THE CAKE OR COPPING OUT

by Brook Sexton

Brook Sexton is a young leader in the National Federation of the Blind. With candor and unflinching self-honesty she shares her journey to belief. Here is what she has to say:

"What can I do to help?" I asked with the intention to do whatever needed to be done to set up for the annual teacher appreciation dinner put on by the youth of my church. I was unprepared for the answer.

"Well, here's a knife. Will you cut the cake?"

Often in these situations I am asked to fill the water pitchers, carry a loaf of bread to the serving table, or set out the paper plates and napkins. Or I am told that everything is under control and here's a chair; sit until dinner starts.

A thousand thoughts rushed through my mind: *Who me—the blind lady?* Sure, I can cut a cake, but not here! Wow, this is what I had wanted all my life, but... You don't ask me to do anything for nine months, and now you want me to... No, I can't. What if I make a mess of it? What should I do? Why that task? Can I?... Can I?...

"No, I really don't think I can do that," I replied. Immediately I was ashamed and disappointed in myself. Here I was saying no, when I constantly go around telling everyone that I can do anything a sighted person can do. But, when put to the test, I crumbled and confirmed their misconceptions about blind people.

I don't know who eventually cut the cake, but that night I realized *I* had to

Brook Sexton

start believing *myself* those words that I kept telling people. I *had* to get out of my comfort zone and participate. After all, I wanted to be treated like one of the leaders—not one of the kids.

So, six months later when the same lady asked me to take the lead in making reindeer for a service project I said yes. I had to gather the materials, demonstrate how to fold the washcloth around the bar of soap, explain how to make the antlers, and where to glue the eyes and nose onto the completed reindeer. This was just as intimidating as cutting that cake, because I had never used a hot glue gun before, let alone in front of ten eager teenage girls. I debated whether or not I should get out of this project by being sick the night of the activity or asking someone else to teach the girls how to make the project. But at the same time, that cake still plagued me.

A couple of days before the event, I found myself sitting on the kitchen floor making reindeer. Throughout the evening, I had an ongoing debate with myself about the reasons I was not going to flake out of this responsibility. As I successfully made the project in the privacy of my home, the negative, poor helpless blind person lost the debate, and I knew I would follow through with the assignment.

Not surprisingly, the activity was a success. The girls understood the steps (which were not difficult at all), and everyone socialized as we made 100 reindeer. We giggled and told stories about past Christmases; we had a great time. No one knew that part of the reason I was so happy was that I had finally stepped out of that comfort zone.

When my sister Amber got married, it was my responsibility to help clean up after the wedding. Those helping with the cleanup were members of my church and have known me all of my life. They knew me when I didn't use a cane, when I let people sit me in a chair instead of helping with chores or projects, and they knew me when I didn't believe in myself. I had not been around those people since I was young, and I wanted them to learn that blind people *could* compete. Therefore, instead of asking timidly, "What can I do to help?" I asked, "What needs to be done?" Among the many things, we needed to vacuum the hall where the reception had been held.

Though I asked where to find the vacuum and set out to accomplish this task, I wasn't sure where to begin. Again, this was not a difficult task, yet I felt some trepidation. However, the difference was that I did not let this fear overpower me. I didn't allow the negative, poor, helpless blind person to participate in the debate. I vacuumed that room and realized my comfort zone was expanding.

Whether it is a cake to cut, a project to demonstrate, or a hall to vacuum I have learned that it is not enough just to say I can do something or even to believe I can do it.

It's essential that I demonstrate through my actions—to myself as well as to others—that I can compete with my sighted peers.

I have learned that the little things that occur each day can build or destroy my own confidence. And the little things that we do each day slowly—but surely—change society's perceptions of the capabilities of blind people.

DUNNS RIVER FALLS

by Ramona Walhof

Ramona Walhof's stories have appeared many times in the pages of the Kernel Books. She has written about sewing, her children, and her grandchildren. But in this story we see Ramona's adventurous side. Here is what she has to say:

The National Federation of the Blind of Colorado announced a cruise as a fundraiser. I ignored it. There were a couple of cruises I would like to do, but this was not really one of them, and it cost more money than I thought I should spend right then. But my friend Sue Wunder told me all the reasons I should go. A lot of my friends were going, she said, and after all I had known her since kindergarten, and since she lives clear across

*Seville Allen and Ramona Walhof enjoy
the falls at Dunns River Falls in Jamaica.*

the country, it would be fun to have her and others along on a vacation. So I said I'd think about it if I could find a roommate. Judy Sanders, another friend, was looking for a roommate. So I would go!

I had very little time to prepare. I was traveling for the NFB quite a bit, and the cruise was right after Christmas. I was busy, and the information from the Cruise Shoppe didn't come until about three weeks before the cruise. That was at Christmastime, and I was still busy. I don't have the skill to look through a "bunch of stuff" on the Internet, so I waited. When I got the information with the cruise tickets, it was largely about tours we could buy at the various ports where we would stop. Well, I wanted to see the people more than the ocean and the fish.

An interesting tour was described in Jamaica. It appeared that we could climb up a waterfall on the Dunns River. If the falls weren't too noisy, that could be fun. Surely, they wouldn't invite tourists to climb up the falls if it was against a powerful current. This sounded like a challenge—a new experience, a chance to meet some Jamaican people perhaps, and something interesting and fun to do.

I mentioned it to my son who has spent some time in the Caribbean. He had not climbed the Falls, but his friends had. He told me it was dangerous. One of his friends turned around part-way up because it was slippery, but the other one climbed all the way to the top. He thought I should not take that tour. Well, I was still interested. I don't think my son was worried primarily about the fact that I am totally blind. More likely, he was considering the fact that I am sixty-two years old and not in top-notch physical condition. But one cannot be sure.

Boarding the ship in Fort Lauderdale was new and interesting. Seeing other members of the Federation was fun. For once, we were not working; we were playing and relaxing. The weather was much warmer than in

*Ramona Walhof (left) and Seville Allen
(right) stand with their tour guide
in the falls.*

Idaho and very pleasant. Learning about the ship was fascinating. I had never been on a large ship before. Learning some of the protocol was educational. Finding out how to get information about what was going on was a learning process.

The first stop was at Key West. We were still in the United States, but the climate was beautiful, and we went to the Blue Cat Store. I needed a canvas bag and got a flashy one. I was happy to look like a tourist since I was one. Kosumel was supposed to be a good place to shop.

We were told that Hurricane Rita had done a lot of damage, but tourism is the primary industry there, so they are really trying to keep going and rebuild. I found a sun hat and some things for my grandchildren and some nice jewelry at good prices. I like to shop and to look at the merchandise. The merchants were happy for us to touch their wares. Many of the shops were in the open air. I got my feet wet in the ocean, but I knew I would have to get wetter than that before the end of the trip.

My friend, Seville Allen, was interested in climbing the Dunns River Falls, so we decided to take a cab there and hire a guide to climb with us. All the pre-scheduled tours were full. We had put off making our arrangements too long.

When we went ashore, we had no difficulty finding a cab driven by a young man named Martin. Fortunately, he spoke excellent English. He was taken with the idea of the two of us climbing the Falls and took it upon himself to find the "best possible guide." We paraded across the area toward the Falls, and Martin took pleasure in calling to his friends that he had "two girlfriends." Both Seville and I are substantially older than this young man, and you couldn't call us exactly slim and trim.

Yet, we were all enjoying the climate and the fun. Martin was as good as his word. He brought a young woman to us and introduced Tomicia. (I am guessing at the spelling.) Tomicia also spoke quite clear English and was happy to guide two blind women on the Falls. So we were off!

She told us that the Falls used to be 600 feet high, but that erosion had lengthened the height. "Now," she said, "you will be climbing 1,000 feet." Were we up to the task? The noise of the Falls was not too great for us to talk to each other. That was a good sign. We could hear other people around us talking a little. We knew that many were climbing the Falls. Some were having picnics. Some were climbing the steps beside the Falls.

When we stepped into the water, it was cool, but not ice cold. I had worn my swimming suit under capris. However, if I took off the capris, I would have to carry them. Therefore, I decided to continue as I was. I had brought a fanny pack containing my passport and a disposable camera. I did not want to get it wet, and Tomicia calmly assured me that it should not be a problem.

Seville and I were on each side of Tomicia. Each of us had a hand at her elbow and a white cane in the other hand. This was fine, but we knew we would also sometimes need to place one hand on a rock or a wall as we climbed the Falls. Tomicia took us to the first rocks in the water and directed first Seville, then me, to step up onto a big rock.

She was there with a steady hand, but she did not try to push or pull us around. This was delightful. Many people on dry, level land push and pull blind individuals, thinking they are "helping" us go somewhere. Tomicia seemed to understand exactly how to assist us in the very best way.

Soon we reached a wall on our left. Tomicia went ahead, telling Seville to follow her. I followed Seville along the wall, climbing up on rocks when they appeared in front of me. I had rented rubber slippers and had good traction. It did not seem slippery. Seville was wearing sneakers and seemed to be doing fine, also.

Then there came a time when there was no wall. Tomicia said that I should wait for her, and she would go ahead with Seville. I did not like standing alone on top of a rock out in the middle of the river. With my cane I found another nice wet rock at a slightly lower level. Standing with one foot on each of these two rocks felt more secure.

At one time I heard Tomicia telling Seville that she had completed the hardest part of the Falls. Later Seville told me that she had some trouble with her knees and was feeling unsure whether she could manage the entire climb. However, Tomicia's reassurance was what she needed. I don't think we had reached the halfway point, but Tomicia clearly believed we could do the entire climb. By then she had had the opportunity to assess our climbing ability. As I look back on it, she doubtless had needed to encourage other tourists who climbed the Falls before us.

At one point I stepped up to a rock about as high as my hips. However, I didn't realize there was a rock protruding toward me lower than the one I was trying to step on. I could have taken two steps more easily if I had checked it out more carefully. I caught my toe on the lower rock and lost my rubber slipper. I did not look forward to finishing the climb without it, and I knew I could not chase it down the Falls. But Tomicia came to my rescue. The slipper had landed on another nice rock. Tomicia returned it to me.

She kept her cool, and I kept mine. I sat right down in the cool water and put it back on, and we continued on our way. Seville must have wondered why Tomicia quickly left her, but she knew by then that Tomicia was using good sense with us, and she also stayed calm.

Sometimes the water was hardly to our ankles. Sometimes it came clear up to our hips. There was current, but not so much that it was frightening. I love water, but I respect it, too. As I became concerned that my passport and camera would get wet, I moved my fanny pack up from my waist to my shoulders.

Perhaps it looked odd, but this was not an ordinary project. As I became thoroughly wet, my capris began to slide down on my wet swimming suit underneath. I had to keep pulling them up, but it still seemed easier than carrying them. These were just a few little details that made the adventure more fun.

At one point Tomicia took us out into the middle of the Falls past a long column of people on the left. It became apparent that there was a larger tour group along the edge. They spoke to us as we passed, and some of them reached out to steady us. They had the wall for support at that time, and we probably looked as precarious as we felt climbing up the middle of the Falls. I have no idea why we were passing that group, but we left them behind. I think most groups made a little better time than Seville and I. We did not hurry.

Then there was a time when Tomicia showed us rocks at our shoulder level with water pouring over them. I thought: "How can we get up these?" Tomicia showed us where to go to one side of them, and there were nice steps right up.

Tomicia also knew good spots for pictures. From time to time she would call to another guide. They did this every day. We were Tomicia's second tour that day. Experience she certainly had, and I have no doubt that quite a few young people have that. How she learned exactly how to guide two blind people I do not know. There is no question, however, that she was a wonderful guide for us. Both Seville and I had a terrific time and will long remember our Dunns River Falls adventure.

The next day we stopped at the Grand Cayman Islands. That was the day for the beach and swimming in the ocean. I went with a group of young Federationists and loved the water and the beach. There were hundreds of coral rocks on the beach and in the ocean—some smooth with wear and some still rough.

It was a fine vacation. Going with friends in the National Federation of the Blind did make it more fun. I met sighted people on the boat and off. That was also fun. All the NFB members did what we liked. My roommate Judy played trivia games and made friends with others who liked to do that. I went to a singles party and swam in the ship's pools.

The crew on the ship must have been surprised to have so many people with white canes and a few guide dogs onboard. They are trained to give service, and they did exactly that. We learned our way around the ship, or at least most of us did. When it was stormy and the ship rocked vigorously, we staggered about as much as the others. I will know how to plan better if I ever take another cruise, but I will never forget this one—especially Dunns River Falls.

OTHER KERNEL BOOKS

You can help us spread the word...

...about our *Braille Readers Are Leaders* contest for blind schoolchildren, a project which encourages blind children to achieve literacy through Braille.

...about our scholarships for deserving blind college students.

...about NFB-NEWSLINE®, a free service that allows blind persons to read the newspaper over the telephone.

...about where to turn for accurate information about blindness and the abilities of the blind.

Most importantly, you can help us by sharing what you've learned about blindness in these pages with your family and friends. If you know anyone who needs assistance with the problems of blindness, please write:

Marc Maurer, President
National Federation of the Blind
1800 Johnson Street, Suite 300
Baltimore, Maryland 21230

Other Ways You Can Help the National Federation of the Blind

Write to us for tax-saving information on bequests and planned giving programs.

OR

Include the following language in your will:

"I give, devise, and bequeath unto National Federation of the Blind, 1800 Johnson Street, Suite 300, Baltimore, Maryland 21230, a District of Columbia nonprofit corporation, the sum of \$_____ (or "___ percent of my net estate" or "The following stocks and bonds:_____") to be used for its worthy purposes on behalf of blind persons."

Your Contributions Are Tax-deductible